PALM READING

FIND OUT YOUR FUTURE

D1295528

PALM READING
FIND OUT YOUR FUTURE

The secrets of character and destiny revealed in the hand:
a practical guide with 200 photographs and illustrations

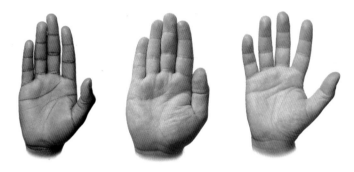

STACI MENDOZA & DAVID BOURNE

southwater

This edition is published by Southwater, an imprint of Anness Publishing Ltd,
Hermes House, 88–89 Blackfriars Road, London SE1 8HA; tel. 020 7401 2077; fax 020 7633 9499

www.southwaterbooks.com; www.annesspublishing.com

If you like the images in this book and would like to investigate using them for publishing, promotions
or advertising, please visit our website www.practicalpictures.com for more information.

UK agent: The Manning Partnership Ltd; tel. 01225 478444; fax 01225 478440; sales@manning-partnership.co.uk
UK distributor: Grantham Book Services Ltd; tel. 01476 541080; fax 01476 541061; orders@gbs.tbs-ltd.co.uk
North American agent/distributor: National Book Network; tel. 301 459 3366; fax 301 429 5746; www.nbnbooks.com
Australian agent/distributor: Pan Macmillan Australia; tel. 1300 135 113; fax 1300 135 103; customer.service@macmillan.com.au
New Zealand agent/distributor: David Bateman Ltd; tel. (09) 415 7664; fax (09) 415 8892

Publisher: Joanna Lorenz
Project Editor: Debra Mayhew
Designer: Nigel Partridge;
Illustrator: Anna Koska
Photographer: John Freeman

ETHICAL TRADING POLICY
Because of our ongoing ecological investment programme, you, as our customer, can have the pleasure and
reassurance of knowing that a tree is being cultivated on your behalf to naturally replace the materials used to make
the book you are holding. For further information about this scheme, go to www.annesspublishing.com/trees

© Anness Publishing Limited 2000, 2008

All rights reserved. No part of this publication may be reproduced, stored in a retrieval system, or transmitted
in any way or by any means, electronic, mechanical, photocopying, recording or otherwise, without
the prior written permission of the copyright holder.

A CIP catalogue record for this book is available from the British Library.

Previously published as *The New Life Library: Palm Reading*

The reader should not regard the recommendations, ideas and techniques expressed and described in this book
as substitutes for the advice of a qualified medical practitioner or other qualified professional. Any use to
which the recommendations, ideas and techniques are put is at the reader's sole discretion and risk.

CONTENTS

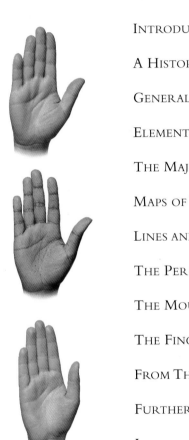

INTRODUCTION	6
A HISTORY OF PALMISTRY	8
GENERAL ASPECTS OF THE HAND	10
ELEMENTAL HANDS	16
THE MAJOR LINES OF THE HAND	18
MAPS OF TIME	32
LINES AND SIGNS OF SPECIAL INTEREST	34
THE PERCUSSIVE OR PALM EDGE	37
THE MOUNTS OF THE HAND	38
THE FINGERS AND THUMB	54
FROM THEORY TO PRACTICE	60
FURTHER INFORMATION	63
INDEX	64

INTRODUCTION

The "hands-on" approach used in palmistry makes it one of the kindest and friendliest methods of divination – used in revealing information about a person's future and characteristics. All the time you are looking into the palm, to interpret the lines and markings found there, you are touching and holding someone's hand. This intimate and caring gesture can have a profound effect in lifting any impersonal barriers to communication: it allows the person to feel comfortable and cared-for as an individual enabling them to open up and bring out whatever is really on their mind at the time.

◀ *The palmistry hand is an ancient teaching tool.*

Before you begin to read someone's palm, it is important to look at both the hands to judge the various changes between childhood and adult life. Take note of whether the person is right- or left-handed, in order to establish the "major" and "minor" hands. The palm-reader reads the major hand (the one used to write with) to find what an individual has made of their life up to

▼ *The hands are used as a gesture of elation.*

▼ *Hands are used to express protection and tenderness.*

▲ *The hennaed Hand of Fatima is an historical Middle Eastern symbol of creation on the hands of women.*

the present time, and what is in store for them in the future. The minor hand reveals the past history and family background and shows what talents or assets are inborn.

Before you begin your reading, choose a peaceful setting that is comfortable both for you and the other person. Try to clear your mind, and then proceed to look clearly at the hands, always listening to your sixth sense or intuition when relaying the information you can uncover. You will also find it helpful to have a notebook (to jot down your observations), a magnifying

glass (to see the palm's markings more clearly) a ruler, and a pair of compasses. Put them within easy reach so that you do not have to interrupt your reading once you have begun.

This book is an introduction to the concept of palmistry, illustrating in detail what to look for in the hand and providing guidance in interpreting what you find. The final section takes you through a complete reading with practical guidelines to help you order your thoughts and communicate them effectively.

Once you have discovered just how much information is on the palm, you are bound to look at hands in a different light. Palmistry is a wonderful way to discover more about yourself as well as your friends and family.

▼ *A handshake or simple touch can mean many things.*

A HISTORY OF PALMISTRY

Palmistry is one of the oldest and most universally practised of all the forms of divination. Its ancient roots lie in the East, where records exist in China from as early as 3200 BC showing that palmistry was regularly practised as a means of divination. In India, Hindus also practised palmistry from a very early date, and developed it as a system called *hastarika* (the "study of the hand with its forms and lines"). Like its counterpart from China, it is still in prominent use today.

From these two ancient sources, palmistry migrated via the trade routes through Persia and the Middle East into the West. The ancient Greeks have left us records of their practice of

▼ The Chiromancer *by Piero della Vecchia is a 17th-century study of the courtiers' fascination for palm reading.*

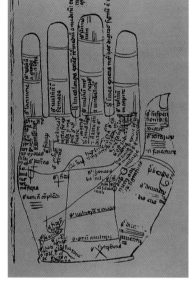

▲ *Early maps of the palm show us historical approaches to palm reading.*

chiromancy (a word which comes from *kheir*, "hand" and *manteia*, "divination"). Aristotle, Pythagoras and Anaxagoras all expounded the benefits of the study of this practice.

Perhaps the most famous exponents of palmistry are the nomadic tribes who roamed across Europe for centuries practising their popular trade.

During the 15th and 16th centuries printed books began to be widely circulated. *Die Kunst Ciromantia* by Johann Hartlieb and *Chyromantiae* by Barthelemy Cocles laid the foundations, and palmistry became a documented practice all over Europe.

After this golden age, interest in palmistry waned until the middle of the 19th century: a period that saw a great revival of interest in all things esoteric. It was restored to public attention by notable figures such as d'Arpentigny, Desbarroles and "Cheiro" (Count Louis von Hamon), who set the salons of London alight with his charismatic consultations given in his Indian room.

It was Cheiro who brought together the various philosophies into a coherent whole. Adding his own ideas, he enabled the practice of palmistry to grow. Since then, it has developed to fit the constraints of the modern world where palmists still practise what is perhaps the most truly human-orientated form of divination.

▶ The Fortune Teller *by Jean Antoine Watteau portrays the spread of palmistry among European gentry.*

GENERAL ASPECTS OF THE HAND

Before studying the lines and markings of the palm itself, some general indications of personality can be drawn from some aspects of the whole hand. This information should be collected as a whole to give you a general picture of the person whose palm you are interpreting. More advanced palmists will also take into consideration the undertones of the skin and the texture of the hand itself.

THE SHAPE OF THE HAND

Ascertain the overall shape of the whole hand by simply holding the hand up with the palm facing you and using an imaginary outline to gauge its shape. The more this process is practised the easier it is for the eye to recognize the shapes. There are four main shapes:

◄ *Conical hand.*

◄ *Pointed hand.*

THE POINTED OR "PSYCHIC" HAND

Narrow hand; middle finger peaks higher than others

Individuals with this shape hand tend to have keen intuitive faculties and a sixth sense, hence its name. Usually very good-looking, they strive for perfection around them and within themselves.

THE CONICAL OR "ARTISTIC" HAND

Gently rounded shape

This shape is so called because people with this type of hand are extremely visual, and have a tendency to artistic and visually-based pursuits; they are sensual by nature. They want to see all the beauty in life, and they see life as something to be enjoyed.

▶ *Square hand.*

THE SQUARE OR "USEFUL" HAND

Square shape

This shape belongs to individuals who need to be needed. They have a logical pattern to their thinking, and usually have a good mechanical sense. They are often very busy physically.

THE SPATULATE OR "NECESSARY" HAND

The palm widens out from a narrow base

These people get things done. They will do whatever is necessary to succeed, and are persistent and bright enough to carry it off. These individuals hate to waste time.

◄ *Spatulate hand.*

THE PROPORTIONS OF THE HAND

Differences in length between the palm and the fingers can usually be seen with the naked eye but if necessary simply measure the difference using a ruler. By holding the ruler lengthwise alongside the whole hand you can assess at a glance the proportions of fingers to palm.

PALM IS LONGER THAN FINGERS

This indicates people who have difficulty in saying no to their whims; people of ideas and dreams who can conjure up great schemes but need to watch out for the "Oh, I'll put it off until tomorrow" syndrome. They are creative, and may be artists or musicians.

◄ *Palm is longer than fingers.*

PALM IS SAME LENGTH AS FINGERS

Very balanced individuals have this balanced hand. They find it relatively easy to cope with the highs and lows in life and are usually stable in character, both mentally and physically. They are determined individuals who have the ability to see things out to the end and have a logical approach to life. They are very fortunate in that they suffer few health problems, mental or physical.

◄ *Palm is same length as fingers.*

▼ *A creative aptitude and dextrous ability is needed to play musical instruments. A person with these abilities is likely to have a palm longer than their fingers.*

▲ *Some talented people use their hands to make beautiful works of art.*

PALM IS SHORTER THAN FINGERS

These individuals will always use their gut intuition to guide them through life. They are very imaginative, spiritual and sensitive personalities. They have a delicate constitution and may suffer health problems.

► *Palm is shorter than fingers.*

FINGER SHAPES

When assessing the shape of the fingers, examine them with the palm facing you looking only at the overall shape of the fingertips while ignoring the shape of the fingernails. Many people will have a mixture of finger shapes so look for the shape which occurs most frequently. Also take into account the settings, spacings and patterns upon the fingers and thumb, all of which are dealt with in a later chapter.

POINTED FINGERTIPS

Finicky, precise personalities, these people have a good eye for colours, shapes and designs. They are refined, with a highly developed aesthetic sense and good taste, evident in their dress and homes.

CONICAL FINGERTIPS

These individuals carry certain instinctive beliefs about themselves and possess a great inner knowledge of other people's circumstances and concerns. They are generally wise souls with a gentle nature, always willing to lend a hand and help out. They are usually very attractive.

SQUARE FINGERTIPS

These people prefer to lead a simple life, with simple pleasures to keep them happy. They are excellent workers, who are always able to make money easily, and so do well in the field of business. They are always fair in their approach and in their dealings with others.

▲ *The homes of people with pointed fingertips are often stylish and tasteful, reflecting their good taste.*

SPATULATE FINGERTIPS

Highly intelligent and witty, these people have a dry sense of humour and are mentally versatile. They enjoy travelling. They are very active and will generally go for a career in which they will work non-stop around the clock. They are adaptable, capable of handling most situations and other people.

◄ *Most people will have more than one shape of fingertip on their hand. Base your reading on the shape which occurs most frequently. Finger shapes (left to right): pointed, conical, square and spatulate.*

HAND THICKNESS

Tilt the hand sideways to gain some idea of its depth and suppleness. The suppleness is difficult to ascertain at first, but with practice you will get used to the feeling of different types of hands and will be able to gauge this with more confidence.

VERY THICK AND VERY HARD

These individuals tend to behave in a very rough and tough manner, following their own basic needs. Their thought processes tend to be crude.

THICK AND HARD

These people have very basic needs: food, shelter and love. Free from ambition, they have no desire to keep up with the rat race.

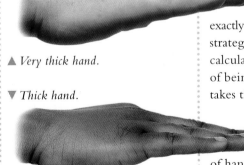

▲ *Very thick hand.*

▼ *Thick hand.*

THICK AND MEDIUM HARD

These people are good workers, always reliable and trustworthy. They will tend to work hard throughout their lives. Life does not come too easily for them, but they usually enjoy it.

THICK AND MEDIUM SOFT

These people work hard and play hard; they really want to enjoy themselves with other people. They need to be needed and like to be useful and relied on.

THICK AND SOFT

These people are artists, poets or musicians, but are not usually very good workers. They tend to dream and ponder on life, rather than getting their hands dirty.

THIN AND VERY HARD

These individuals know exactly what they want. They possess strategic skills and can be quite calculating. They may be accused of being cold, but in fact it just takes time to get to know them.

THIN AND HARD

People with this kind of hand tend to be selfish by

▲ *Thin hand.*

▼ *Very thin hand.*

nature and self-opinionated. They are possessive and stubborn and do not make friends easily, although the alliances they do make are usually for life.

THIN AND SOFT

These people love to have a good time, and are always the last to leave a party. They do not have much willpower and find it difficult to say "no" to people, so they are susceptible to physical temptations such as affairs or one night stands.

THIN AND VERY SOFT

These individuals have a keen intuition, but also have a tendency to focus on the negative, which may lead them to react harshly or snap at other people. They can even be prone to problems such as depression, morbidity and paranoia.

THE SIZE OF THE HAND

Small, average or large hands may appear a strange distinction at first. When ascertaining the size of the hand, however, you should consider it in relation to the person's size and build. Ask yourself if it is in proportion. For example, a small person who has small hands would be considered to have hands of average size. The hands of a tall and broadly built man might be larger, but if they look dainty compared to the rest of his body you should consider them as small.

▼ *People with large hands are often surprisingly dextrous.*

VERY SMALL HANDS

Individuals with proportionally very small hands tend to be free thinkers. They often have a strong sense of moral politics and will stick firmly to their beliefs. Consequently, they like to fight for the underdog against dishonesty and injustice. This passion, however, may lead to a tendency not to listen to the other side of a story, so their support can be misguided. If a man has exceptionally small hands in relation to his size, it can indicate a cruel side to his nature.

▼ *Very small hands are not only petite but often delicate to the touch.*

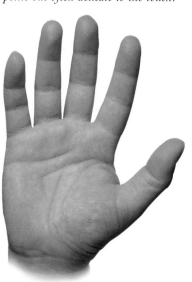

SMALL HANDS

Individuals who have proportionally small hands are ideas people. They often come up with bright and broad-reaching ideas, but need others to help carry them through. They make very good committee members and fundraisers because they possess an ability to gather the support and enthusiasm of others. They are usually very dear and sweet in nature, and would not hurt a fly.

▼ *Small hands are petite but have larger fingers than the very small hand.*

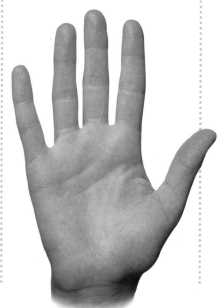

AVERAGE HANDS

People with average size hands are down-to-earth individuals who usually possess good common sense and moderate views on life. Such people have balanced, healthy attitudes and are good-natured when dealing with other people. Any mental or physical problems are usually easily overcome.

▼ *The average hand may not catch your eye but it is a good, solid shape with pleasing proportions.*

LARGE HANDS

People with large hands have a, perhaps surprising, aptitude for doing fiddly things with great patience, and may use this talent to earn their living. They have excellent analytical talents and are mentally strong and good-natured. They can usually be found figuring out detailed projects or pursuing hobbies.

▼ *Large hands are wider than average hands.*

VERY LARGE HANDS

These individuals are very bright mentally. They love trivia and mental exercises which sharpen their minds. They can be the mavericks and trendsetters and are unlikely to accept the status quo. They often possess a great strategic ability. They like to be constantly in charge of life, and object to being told what to do.

▼ *Very large hands are unusual.*

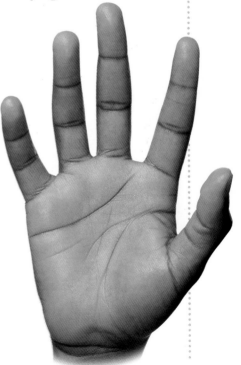

ELEMENTAL HANDS

There are four basic types of the elemental hand: water, air, fire and earth. Assessing this aspect gives an overview of a person's character based on astrological principles. This then complements the detailed interpretation of the palm and fingers. The elemental hand often corresponds with the individual's astrological sign.

▼ *The Water Hand indicates an artistic, sensitive character.*

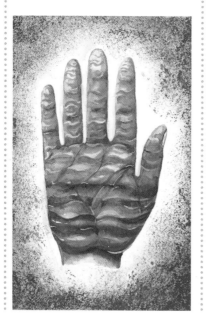

THE WATER HAND

A delicate structure with long fingers and a long palm. Features a fine mesh of linear markings

Often, though not always, the water hand belongs to those people born under one of the three water signs: Cancer, Pisces and Scorpio. They possess emotional natures, with very sensitive and sensual personalities. They are often artistic, enigmatic, esoteric and intuitive. The water hand usually accompanies an attractive face with large, intense eyes and soft lips. These people have a love of music, art and culture, and seek relationships: they need to belong to someone or something, in order to feel content with their lives.

THE AIR HAND

A robust hand structure with long fingers and a fleshy, though square, palm. Well-defined linear markings

The air hand frequently belongs to those born under one of the three air signs: Libra, Gemini and Aquarius. They are intellectual in their pursuits and possess well-

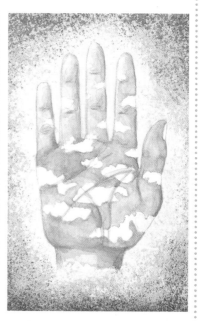

▲ *The Air Hand indicates a strong-minded and well-balanced character.*

balanced minds. They are literate and not overly sensitive to visual stimuli. They need facts and figures to help guide their decision making, and they look for mental challenges. They are strong-minded individuals with a powerful sense of self. For their relationships to work and not become bogged down or boring, these people need to retain their independence and personal freedom. They need a strong sense of self to be content in life.

THE FIRE HAND

A lively hand structure with short fingers and a long palm. The hand features lively linear markings. Often, though not always, the fire hand belongs to those people

▼ *Individuals with a Fire Hand tend to be fiery characters who like responsibility as long as it involves action and excitement.*

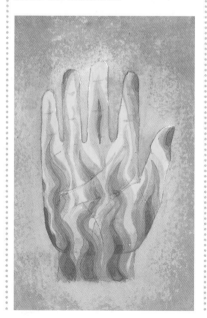

born under one of the three fire signs: Aries, Sagittarius and Leo. These individuals have strong instincts, and act on gut feelings. Often they are assertive and quick to rise, but also quick to cool down.

They are usually very active individuals who prefer action to excuses; they need to be kept busy, otherwise they are easily bored. These people can handle the stresses of a battle but cannot always cope with the more mundane responsibilities of life. They like to be life's leaders and do not enjoy following on behind others.

THE EARTH HAND

A heavy, thick hand structure with short fingers and a coarse, square palm. The lines on the palm are few but are deeply incised The earth hand frequently belongs to people born under one of the three earth signs: Capricorn, Taurus and Virgo. They are well-balanced, practical and logical by nature and so make good problem solvers. They have an inherent wisdom. They are sure-footed in their dealings with people and have a useful

▲ *Individuals with an Earth Hand are down-to-earth, reliable characters with a useful ability to detect fakes and swindlers.*

ability to detect fakes or liars. Once committed to a personal relationship, they are normally very devoted.

Earth types need a purpose in life and usually feel a need to be relied upon in order to be content. They are not afraid of, nor do they mind, good, honest hard work in order to reach their goals.

THE MAJOR LINES OF THE HAND

There are six major lines of the hand. At least three will be found on every hand, and some people will have all six. Remember that, whether you find only three or all six, the hand must be interpreted as a whole. So, while you are considering these major lines, you will still be considering the shape and size of the hand, the mounts, other lines, and the fingers. The major lines are normally assessed by the palm-reader in their order of importance, so you should follow the order given below.

You may find it difficult to decide whether a particular line is actually missing or is merely very faint. Try to ask a professional reader for advice if this is likely to cause anxiety.

LIFE LINE OR "VITAL LINE"
As the most vital line in the hand, the life line is usually read first by the palm-reader. It deals with the length of life, the strength and generalities of life and family ties. It is never absent.

HEAD LINE OR "CEREBRAL LINE"
This line deals with the mind, indicating weak or strong mentalities, possible career directions, and intuitive and creative faculties. Serious mental illness may be indicated by its absence, although this condition is very rare.

HEART LINE OR "MESAL LINE"
This line deals with love and the emotions. It indicates degrees of contentment and happiness in life, and shows the kinds of relationships people have with others. The longer the line and the more it reaches towards the Jupiter finger, the longer a

◀ *The major lines of the hand are the basis for the palm-reader's first impression. The palmist will then assess the finer lines and markings to fine tune their reading.*

SUN LINE

HEART LINE

HEAD LINE

MERCURY LINE

FATE LINE

LIFE LINE

relationship is likely to last. Its absence is rare, but it can be a grave omen. If you detect this line be tactful with your subject and ask a professional reader for advice.

FATE LINE OR "LINE OF LUCK" This line deals with career, work and ambition. It is concerned with the directional force of life,

▶ *These three palms illustrate the differences in the length and position*

social standing and the public aspects of people's lives. It frequently takes the place of the line of the Sun.

LINE OF THE SUN OR APOLLO, ALSO KNOWN AS THE "LINE OF FORTUNE AND BRILLIANCY" This line deals with luck, talent, and money. It augurs success and, possibly, fame. Any visible Sun

of the major lines on the hand. Look very carefully: are you able to

line is good luck. The longer it is, the greater the luck. It often takes the place of the fate line.

LINE OF MERCURY. ALSO CALLED THE "HEALTH LINE" OR LIVER LINE This line deals with health issues which may be hereditary. It is often absent, but this is auspicious as it indicates good health.

recognize the lines on each of the three hands illustrated?

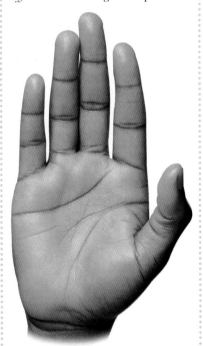
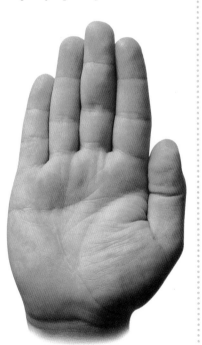
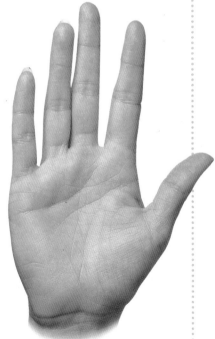

THE LIFE LINE

The life line is the measure of vitality and life force. It deals with the length and strength of life, family ties and the

▼ *The main life line may be supplemented by the Mars line, worry lines and loyalty lines.*

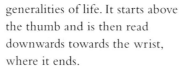

generalities of life. It starts above the thumb and is then read downwards towards the wrist, where it ends.

You may notice one or more thin horizontal lines cutting directly across the life line. These indicate slight obstacles at a given time period.

1 LIFE LINE CLOSE TO THE THUMB
This indicates someone who has a close relationship with their family and is content with family life. They are happy spending time at home, with no great urge to travel around the world, and are not ambitious. It can also mean a heavy family commitment. These people are sensitive and cautious.

2 LIFE LINE LIES TOWARDS THE MIDDLE OF THE HAND
If the life line skirts the thumb in a wide arc and rests more in the middle of the hand, it indicates a person who wants to achieve great things and break new ground. They will have a keen sense of adventure and want to travel.

3 LINE ENDS TOWARDS THUMB SIDE OF WRIST
When the life line veers around the thumb to end at the side of the wrist, this indicates an individual who yearns for home, and wants to end their years on home ground.

4 LINE ENDS TOWARDS OPPOSITE SIDE OF WRIST
When the end of the life line veers away from the thumb towards the opposite side of the hand, this indicates a person who will emigrate, or move away from their family, culture or country.

5 LINE STARTS AT BASE OF JUPITER
When the life line starts at the base of the mount of Jupiter, below the index finger, the individual seeks a change of lifestyle for the better. They are strong-willed and very ambitious, willing to conquer obstacles to achieve their goals.

6 LINE STARTS AT SIDE OF HAND NEAR JUPITER
This is similar to the previous position, and indicates people who are ambitious and will

▲ *The position of the life line indicates those with an adventurous spirit and those happy to remain close to home.*

single-mindedly achieve success. They are proud characters who make good leaders.

7 LINE CUTS CLOSE TO THUMB

When the line cuts very close to the thumb, this indicates someone who is living a restricted life: they may be under a strong religious or cultural influence at home. It may also mean that they have been imprisoned at some point, or have lived in the same town all their life.

8 BREAKS IN THE LIFE LINE

Breaks signify starts and stops in life resulting from big changes such as marriage, divorce, or the death of a close relative.

9 DOUBLE LIFE LINE

A double life line signifies a dual existence, and can mean any of three things: the person may be one of a pair of twins; they may have a guardian angel watching over them; or they may lead a double life, such as a mother who cares for four children during the day and works in a club at night.

10 EFFORT LINE

When the life line veers upwards towards the mount of Saturn, a person is putting great effort into their life, working hard and not taking no for an answer. But this does not necessarily mean success.

11 SUCCESS LINE

When the life line veers upward towards the mount of the Sun, below the third finger, this indicates great success and good financial fortune. It may also be a sign of fame.

12 MARS LINE

This line, running inside the life line, indicates that the person has a guardian angel or protective spirit looking after them here on earth; this is usually a very close relative or friend who has died.

13 WORRY LINES

Horizontal lines creased in the pad of the thumb indicate stresses and worries. The deeper the lines the more serious the worries. If the lines are many and faint, the individual is prone to anxiety and is nervous by nature.

14 LOYALTY LINES

Vertical lines creased in the pad of the thumb indicate loyalty to family and friends.

▼ *Family-oriented individuals are likely to have a life line situated close to their thumb.*

THE HEAD LINE

This line deals with the mind, indicating weak or strong mentalities, possible career directions, and intuitive and creative faculties. When reading

▼ *The head line deals with an individual's strength of character.*

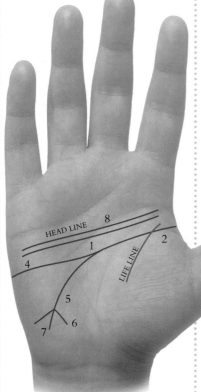

the head line, you should look first to see whether the line is thin (faint) or thick (wide and deep). A thin line indicates a person who is highly strung emotionally, and can at times be volatile or unstable. A thick line indicates someone who is methodical. They seem to lack enthusiasm and drive at times; they are solid and sound but stubborn in nature and cannot be swayed by the opinions of others.

1 LINE STARTS HIGH NEAR JUPITER

A head line that starts on the mount of Jupiter, under the index finger, indicates an ambitious individual who is a self-starter and very focused. They can be very competitive and determined in their efforts to achieve their goals in life.

2 HEAD AND LIFE LINES TIED

This usually indicates an individual beset by doubt and confusion which leads to a lack of independence. They are very involved with the family. They have little self-confidence and

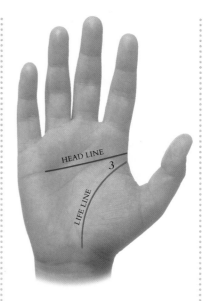

▲ *The head line may be positioned separate from the life line.*

doubt their own abilities. This is often as a result of their upbringing or early environment.

3 HEAD LINE SEPARATE FROM LIFE LINE

When the head line is clearly segregated from the life line, it indicates an individual who possesses great independence and self-will. This is a free thinker who does not follow others but will make their own road in life.

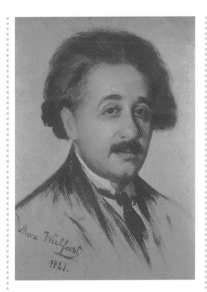

▲ *An eminent scientist like Albert Einstein is likely to have a double head line. Not surprisingly, it is a rare mark.*

4 LINE CUTS STRAIGHT ACROSS PALM
When the head line touches both sides of the palm, this indicates a self-centred individual who has the ability to stay very focused on their needs and goals. They must have secure material foundations, such as house ownership, insurance policies, and a healthy bank balance. The good news is that they are good citizens and will often give to charity.

5 LINE DIPS DOWNWARD IN PALM, MAKING AN ARCH
This indicates a very sensitive sensitive individual with a highly developed intuition. They are imaginative and perhaps rather eccentric. This may lead them to artistic pursuits or into a profession that involves caring for others.

6 THE "WRITER'S FORK"
A head line that splits in three directions at the end (like a chicken's foot) indicates an intuitive nature, similar to the previous example.

People with this characteristic are inclined to communicate cerebral ideas, thoughts and information to others by using their hands. They are likely to be writers, journalists or computer programmers.

7 THE "COMMUNICATOR'S DIVIDE"
When the head line divides into a two-pronged ending, it indicates a person who has great communication skills, and is an able public speaker. They may work in radio or television, as a professional after-dinner speaker or be an actor or singer.

8 THE DOUBLE-HEADED LINE
Two head lines lying close together indicate an individual with outstanding mental abilities. The double-headed line is so rare that when it does exist the person is likely to be in a very studious and analytically-driven career, such as an eminent mathematician, scientist or other scholar.

▼ *If the head line divides at the end into two prongs it indicates an individual with a good public presence.*

THE HEART LINE

This line deals with all matters relating to the heart: love, romantic interests, and relationships with family and friends. It also indicates the nature of those relationships: whether they are likely to be steady or stormy, short term or long term. In general, the heart line deals with a person's emotional and romantic life.

▼ *The heart line is an indicator of the nature of your emotional life.*

1 LINE LOW IN THE HAND

The heart line starts below the underside of the knuckles in the palm. These individuals are lovers; feminine and romantic, they believe in love and are looking for "fairy-tale" perfection. In matters of the heart they can become perfectionists and expect too much from their partners. This can lead to them feeling let down.

2 LINE HIGH IN THE HAND

The heart line starts on or above the underside of the knuckles in the palm, and appears to rest near the base of the fingers. These individuals are extremely sensitive to what others think of them and can be quite destructive with their self-criticism. They tend to be very reserved with their emotions.

▲ *A fairy-tale view of romance is the individual's driving force in life when their heart line drops low in the hand. They may be disappointed.*

3 END OF LINE VEERS TOWARDS MIDDLE OR INDEX FINGERS

This indicates a dominant and demanding person, who expresses their emotions bluntly. Someone whose line veers towards Saturn will have a very contented family life. They keep family members close to them both physically and in their heart.

Veering towards Jupiter, the heart line indicates a person who is very successful in love. They will end their years in love, and being loved.

4 SHORT, HIGH LINE
This person's loyalties and morals are expendable: they believe that sex is the answer. If they are feeling unloved or neglected, or if someone pays a lot of attention to them, they can give themselves over too easily.

5 SHORT, LOW LINE
This individual cannot be faithful; they think that sex is a game or a sport. They

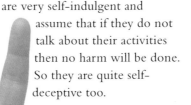

are very self-indulgent and assume that if they do not talk about their activities then no harm will be done. So they are quite self-deceptive too.

6 HEART LINE DROPS DOWN TO TOUCH HEAD AND LIFE LINES
This person wants the best of both worlds: to be happy both at home and at work. They need love but also have a strong sense of independence. At times they can feel divided between family and career. More often they will find a way to juggle both and find a happy medium in their own way.

▼ *The heart line can indicate who is likely to love and be loved into old age.*

▲ *If the heart line touches both the head and life lines, the individual will be good at juggling the often conflicting demands of their family and career.*

7 LINE RUNS STRAIGHT ACROSS THE PALM
A heart line which runs in an almost straight line right across the palm of the hand indicates a humanitarian with a great sense of purpose in life. This type of person will put a great deal of time and effort into working hard for the good of the community. He or she will experience great luck in life due to their selfless nature.

THE FATE LINE

This line deals with career, work, ambition, and the direction of a person's life, beginning from their childhood. It also indicates the

▼ Career, work and degree of ambition can all be deduced by the position of the fate line.

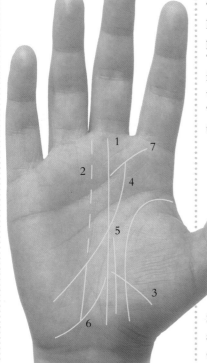

person's faith in their own abilities. It is read from its starting point at the bottom of the palm, near the wrist, and leads up the palm towards the base of the fingers. It ends in varying positions between the index and middle fingers.

1 FATE LINE RUNS VERTICALLY UP THE MIDDLE OF THE PALM

This indicates an individual who has a keen sense of direction and purpose in their life and career. They have known what they want in life from an early age and are very likely to achieve their aims. This line could also indicate that they will pass down their trade or business to their family members.

2 BREAKS IN THE FATE LINE

When the fate line is full of breaks, starts and stops, it indicates an individual who has had many changes in their life and career. Since they have never really been able to become fully involved in one project or in a single career, they may well only be able to achieve mediocre success.

▲ Some individuals have a keen sense of purpose in their life. This is apparent when the fate line is deep, unbroken up the middle of the palm.

3 FATE LINE BEGINS BY VEERING AWAY FROM, OR TOUCHING, THE LIFE LINE

Family commitments were important early in the life of this individual. Before they reach middle-age they will have great family responsibilities or will be heavily involved in a family business. They tend not to want to travel and will tend to stay close to home in later life.

4 LINE STARTS ON LUNAR MOUNT, ON EDGE OF PALM
When the fate line starts from the side of the palm opposite the thumb, it normally indicates an independet individual who will break away from the family

▼ *If a strong fate line veers upwards towards the Jupiter finger the individual's leadership qualities and drive for success will be to the fore.*

traditions in their life and career. It may also indicate someone who is likely to move overseas to work.

5 LINE OF MILIEU
If a separate line runs vertically alongside the fate line for a short distance, it indicates outside pressures or responsibilities for the person concerned. These may be slowing down the individual's way forward, so that they are thwarted in their aims and ambitions. Fortunately this normally lasts only for that period of time.

6 INFLUENCE LINES
If short lines shoot off in a feathering motion from the fate line and veer upwards, they indicate positive influences from other people, whether business associates or family and friends. When the feathery lines veer downwards, they indicate negative influences from other people.

7 LINE ENDS VEERING UPWARDS INTO JUPITER FINGER
This indicates a great ambition and the individual will be successful. They possess great

▲ *Too much pressure could be adversely affecting an individual's work, if a line of milieu runs along their fate line.*

determination and keen leadership qualities. The will to win is second nature.

DOUBLE LINE
A double fate line means one individual with two careers. For example, this could be a person may be running two companies or have one job in the daytime and a different one in the evening. Either way, this dynamic person will have great reserves of energy.

THE SUN LINE

Also known as the line of Apollo, this line deals with luck, success in life, talents, and money. The Sun line is seldom seen below the heart line. The longer the line, the more luck will be found. Two or three lines together also increase a person's chance of luck and good fortune.

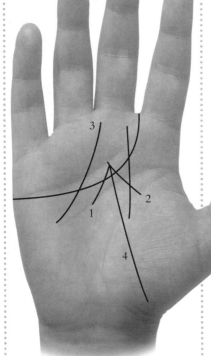

▼ *The Sun line is a fortunate line to have as it indicates almost certain good fortune and a charmed life.*

1 SHORT LINE

When the Sun line is short (anything less than 1cm/½in is considered short), it indicates an individual who has so far been unable to achieve their goals and dreams in life, never quite getting that big break. As any Sun line is a good omen, this individual stands a good chance of finding fortune later in life.

2 CRESCENT-SHAPED LINE VEERS TOWARDS THUMB

This individual works very hard to achieve their goals. No one else does the work for them, and, as a result of this self-reliance, they are quite capable of holding on to their achievements.

3 CRESCENT-SHAPED LINE VEERS AWAY FROM THUMB

This line is a good omen if the individual works in the public eye

▲ *Good fortune will come naturally to the lucky individuals who have a Sun line on their palm.*

as it indicates public prestige, and possibly eventual fame, in recognition of their talents.

4 LONG LINE RUNS VERTICALLY

A long Sun line (anything over 2.5cm/1in is considered long in the hand) indicates a gilded life, with good luck falling into one's lap. Life will come very easily and successfully for this individual, and happiness will follow them all their days.

THE MERCURY LINE

This line is also known as the health or liver line as it deals with health issues, including those that

▼ *The Mercury line is also referred to as the health or liver line. It can indicate good or poor health or an intuitive nature.*

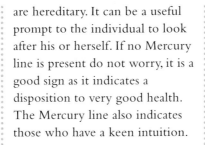

are hereditary. It can be a useful prompt to the individual to look after his or herself. If no Mercury line is present do not worry, it is a good sign as it indicates a disposition to very good health. The Mercury line also indicates those who have a keen intuition.

1 MERCURY LINE CUTS ACROSS LIFE LINE

This indicates a weakened constitution. It is a clear sign of hereditary illness in the family, such as diabetes, heart disease or arthritis. This individual needs to pay special attention to their health in order to combat the likelihood of this kind of illness. (It must be stressed that this line does not show the possibility of a fatal illness.)

2 INTUITION LINE

A Mercury line which runs in a reversed crescent shape indicates a strong sixth sense. It is always present in the hand of the highly intuitive, such as clairvoyant individuals who use their natural insight to guide them through life rather like a compass. These are people who

▲ *A long and happy life is predicted when the Mercury line does not touch the life line.*

have a deep interest in all things esoteric. They are peace-loving and do not like loud noises, big changes or chaos.

3 MERCURY LINE DOES NOT TOUCH LIFE LINE

This is an extremely fortunate line to have in the palm. It indicates very good health and longevity, together with success in business ventures, and good financial fortune.

MARKS ON THE THREE PRINCIPAL LINES

As you read along the major lines of the palm – the life, head and heart lines – you are likely to come across various markings

▼ *Life, head and heart lines*

HEART LINE

HEAD LINE

LIFE LINE

created by the many small lines that cross or abut them. These may include distinctive shapes, such as stars and squares, which will help you in your reading. It must be said that none of these markings imply anything grave or fatal, they simply indicate stresses or irritations, indeed some are signs of protection or good fortune. Similar markings appear on the mounts of the palm, and their meanings are explained in the later section on the mounts.

BARS AND DOTS

These signify interruptions or hindrances that are preventing the individual from moving forward in a given area. There will be hard work involved in recovering momentum, and willpower must be kept up throughout this period of interruptions.

CROSS

This is a sign of a more significant or longer lasting problem such as divorce or the loss of a job or home. On the life line, one cross may indicate a

▲ *Bars (above) and dots (below).*

non-fatal accident in early life or childhood. Two crosses indicate an individual who is sensuous in nature and willing to learn from others. Lots of crosses at the end of the life line can indicate poverty or ill health in old age.

SQUARE

This is a wonderful marking to have; it represents protection and good health, and indicates "getting away with it", or being saved at the last minute. A square containing a cross is a sign of preservation: there will be danger but it will not be harmful. Any square on the life line is good as it indicates safety from danger.

▼ *Cross*

▲ *Square*

▲ *Chain*

CHAIN

This marking indicates confusion, and come on to the lines when someone is trying to do too much at once and spreading their energy too thinly.

ISLAND

An island is a sign that the person's energy temporarily diverges in two directions. The mark shows that the individual has bitten off more than they can chew, but also shows they have the ability to pull it all back together. On the life line, islands indicate serious but treatable illnesses.

▼ *The islands on the palm offer a temporary respite from a situation.*

▲ *A tassel on one of the lines indicates that our reserves of strength have been dissipated.*

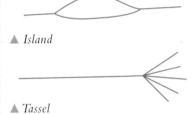

▲ *Island*

▲ *Tassel*

TASSEL

This mark appears at the end of a line and indicates a scattering of the power of the line. On the life line it shows weakened health or life force at the end of life. On the heart line it indicates weakened relationships or an absence of relationships. On the head line it shows that the person is weakened mentally, and possibly even mentally confused.

▲ *Fork*

FORK

A fork in a major line shows increased possibilities of success in life, love or career.

STAR

On the life line, this can indicate the gain (birth) or loss (death) of a relative. For each gain there is a loss and vice versa.

CIRCLES

On the life line, a circle could indicate problems with the eyes.

▼ *Star (left) and Circle (right)*

▼ *The celestial stars are mirrored in the palm.*

MAPS OF TIME

Palms can be divided into time maps that are used to give the palm-reader a clearer idea about when events and situations will take place. They are drawn by dividing the life, fate or head lines on the palm into short sections that roughly correspond to periods of years to give a time frame for events in a person's life. The periods are often gauged by marking the increments of time directly on to the hand with a pen guided only by the naked eye. If you do not have much experience of reading these maps, it is probably safer to mark the increments directly on the hand using a pair of compasses.

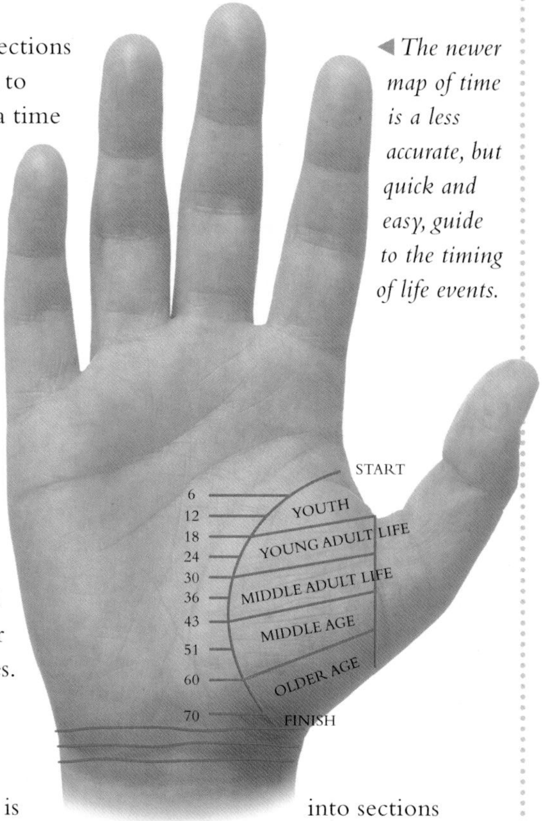

OLDER MAP OF TIME

The older map is used to interpret the ages in the life and head lines. The line is broken down

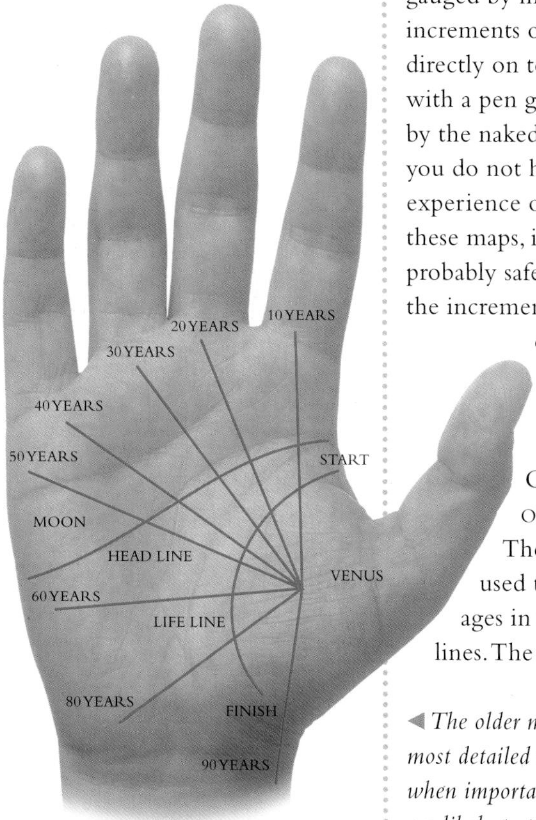

◄ The older map of time gives the most detailed readings. It can show when important life-changing events are likely to take place.

20 YEARS 10 YEARS
30 YEARS
40 YEARS
50 YEARS   START
MOON
HEAD LINE   VENUS
60 YEARS
LIFE LINE
80 YEARS   FINISH
90 YEARS

◄ The newer map of time is a less accurate, but quick and easy, guide to the timing of life events.

START
6
12   YOUTH
18
24   YOUNG ADULT LIFE
30
36   MIDDLE ADULT LIFE
43
51   MIDDLE AGE
60
        OLDER AGE
70   FINISH

into sections which represent increments of ten years. Starting from a middle point at the heart of the thumb pad, divide the life line as shown in the diagram. Begin the reading at the start of the life line, just above the thumb, and move downwards.

▲ *The hand can give a time frame for events in a person's life.*

NEWER MAP OF TIME

This is used to interpret the ages on the life line only. It is a more general, and therefore less precise, way of measuring time on the palm and is often used as a quick reference guide to the timing of events in a life. The life line is broken down roughly into increments of six years. Although more generalized than the older map, this works on the same basis. By reading from the start of the life line, the palm-reader gets a quick idea of the timing of events in the individual's life. If necessary, they can then use the older map of time to look at certain points in depth, giving a more accurate picture of when events are likely to take place.

AGEING MAP OF TIME

This guide to ageing is extremely useful in judging the timing of events and occurrences indicated on the fate line, such as changes of job or career, or a spell of good fortune. The Sun line is also divided into a time frame. It works on a similar basis to the

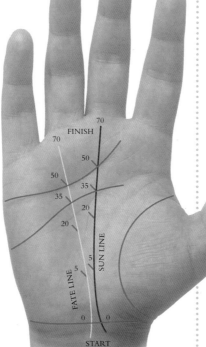

▲ *Important life-changing events, such as the birth of a baby, can be predicted using the Older and Newer Maps of Time.*

other two maps but, here, you take the point at the beginning of the fate line, just above the wrist, and work towards the base of the fingers. The increments on this map are uneven. The ages are: 5, 20, 35, 50 and 70. The Sun line can be read in a similar fashion.

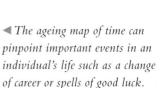

◄ *The ageing map of time can pinpoint important events in an individual's life such as a change of career or spells of good luck.*

LINES AND SIGNS OF SPECIAL INTEREST

Special-interest lines complement the major lines of the palm. They are each unique in their meaning and everyone has at least one, although some people have all of them. They give valuable additional information to

▼ *Individuals with a line of Mars present will often work in the field of safety and protection of others.*

◀ *The line of Mars is a sign of courage.*

the reader about an individual's character, personality and situation, whether it is an indication of courage, psychic ability or a long-lasting romantic commitment.

HEART LINE
HEAD LINE
LINE OF MARS

THE LINE OF MARS
Situated on the side of the palm, between the heart and head line, this line indicates great courage. People who have this line make excellent protectors – it is often to be found on courageous military leaders.

THE RASCETTES, OR "BRACELETS OF LIFE"
These lines are found running across the underside of the wrist just below the palm of the hand, and this is one of the most important areas to check for longevity. The lines can be very

◀ *The rascettes indicate longevity.*

faint or very deep, or somewhere in between. Their depth does not matter; it is the number of lines that counts:
• 1 rascette is equal to 15–35 years of life
• 2 rascettes are equal to 35–55 years of life
• 3 rascettes are equal to 55–85 years of life
• 4 rascettes are equal to 85–105 years of life.

THE RASCETTES

THE GIRDLE OF VENUS
This can either be one continuous line forming the shape of an upturned crescent moon, or made up of two lines. This marking indicates an individual who can

THE GIRDLE OF VENUS

▶ *The girdle of Venus is a sign of a soft nature.*

▲ *Those who care for others will have sympathy lines on their palms.*

empathize with the sorrows of others. Unfortunately, this can lead to them becoming too involved and this can sometimes lead to depression. On a lighter note, these individuals often need to reach for the tissue box when

SYMPATHY LINE

◄ *Sympathy lines are straight, never curved.*

they are watching a sad film on the television.

SYMPATHY LINES
These lines are always straight and are angled upwards. They indicate a caring nature. They can be found on the hands of nurses, doctors and people who feel a strong need to alleviate pain and suffering in others.

MEDICAL STIGMATA
This mark, which is found on the hand of a healer, is made up of no fewer than three lines, with a slash cutting through the middle of them. People with these lines have a healing touch or healing hands. They may be doctors, nurses or other professional carers.

HEALING OR MEDICAL STIGMATA

RING OF SOLOMON
A ring around the mount of Jupiter, which starts at the side of the index finger

◄ *Medical stigmata indicate professional carers.*

◄ *The ring of Solomon can be a sign of psychic ability.*

RING OF SOLOMON

and sweeps around to end between the first and second fingers, indicates wisdom and a deep interest in the occult, the supernatural and other psychic phenomena. On a less psychic level, the ring of Solomon indicates someone who has good leadership skills, is very good at managing people, and will usually achieve success in life.

RING OF SATURN
This semicircular mark beneath the middle finger is rarely found. Whether it is continuous or made up of two or more lines, it seems to isolate and overemphasize the negative Saturnian qualities. Someone with this line will tend to be too serious about life and its problems, and this may lead to depression at times.

RING OF SATURN

▶ *The ring of Saturn is a very rare marking.*

◀ *Look for the mystic cross on the hands of tarot or palm-readers.*

THE MYSTIC CROSS

This marking indicates someone who is naturally talented, possessing a sixth sense and well developed intuition. This is an individual who is keenly interested in the occult sciences, such as the tarot, palmistry, runes and magic.

THE MYSTIC CROSS

PLAIN OF MARS

This is the area in the centre of the palm of the hand. The plain of Mars shows how sensitive an individual is. In most people, this area will appear concave. If it is slightly raised, or even flat, it is therefore called "high". Only if it is very indented is it defined as "low".

AVERAGE PLAIN OF MARS

When the area is slightly concave, it indicates that the person is balanced emotionally, with good sensibilities and a practical approach to life.

SHALLOW PLAIN OF MARS

Individuals with this kind of palm can be stubborn, proud and overbearing. They are single-minded and can do one thing at a time very well. Their lack of sensitivity, however, can make them unaware of the problems of other people around them.

DEEP PLAIN OF MARS

These individuals will always try to help others, and are highly sensitive to other people's opinions and feelings. They feel other people's pain very personally, and make strong efforts not to upset or offend anyone. If the plain of Mars is too low, it can indicate a tendency towards depression.

▼ *Deep plain of Mars (below) and shallow plain of Mars (bottom).*

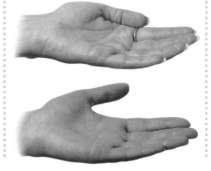

▲ *99.9% of people have marriage lines present which represent serious relationships as well as marriage.*

LINES OF MARRIAGE OR UNION

There may be one line, indicating one serious involvement and commitment, or two or more lines indicating additional emotional involvements. The longer the line horizontally, the longer the relationship.

LINES OF MARRIAGE

▶ *Lines of marriage or union.*

THE PERCUSSIVE OR PALM EDGE

The edge of the palm is a unique area of the hand. It is not a part of the palm itself but rests at the outside edge of the hand. When interpreting this area, take into account that this is the aspect of the individual's personality that is projected to the outside world and shows how others may view them. Have the palm facing you when considering this area.

ACTIVE PERCUSSIVE

This person is usually always busy, with a very active social life. Ever the perfectionist, they search for the best that they can achieve. However, they can have a highly strung nature and be prone to nervousness. These active people are often very physically attractive.

◄ Active percussive edge.

◄ Independent percussive edge.

► Creative percussive edge.

INDEPENDENT PERCUSSIVE

This person is independent and follows their own instincts. They will usually be leaders. They have good intuitive faculties.

CREATIVE PERCUSSIVE

This individual tends to be colourful, with a great imagination and creative tendencies; they set their own trends. They have a knack for creating attractive domestic surroundings.

PHYSICAL PERCUSSIVE

This person has excellent physical health with a physique designed for sport and endurance. They are usually involved in physical activities, such as gardening, walking and sport. They need to feel useful and productive.

INTELLECTUAL PERCUSSIVE

This person prefers mental activity to physical. They are problem solvers with an analytical nature. They tend to be weak physically and need to take rests inbetween bouts of exertion.

▼ Physical percussive edge (left) and intellectual percussive edge (right).

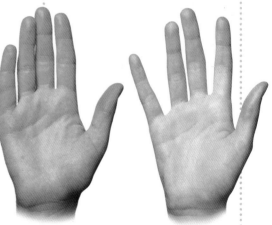

THE MOUNTS OF THE HAND

The fleshy mounds present in different segments of the palm are called the mounts on the hand. Personality types and even physical traits are indicated by the dominant mount. The predominance of one particular mount is found by looking at the palm from various angles and taking note of which mount is raised higher than the others. As the mounts of Venus and the Moon are the widest, it is important that you compare the height rather than the width to establish dominance. A later section, The Mounts Combined, looks at the effect of having two mounts of equal dominance and explores the personality types indicated by each combination.

When looking at the mounts on the palm, the reader usually works clockwise beginning with the mount of Venus.

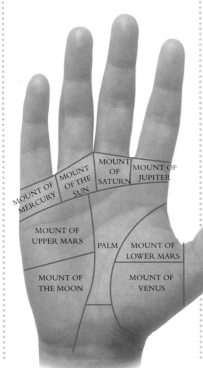

▼ The mounts of the hand indicate personality types and can even predict physical characteristics.

MOUNT OF MERCURY
MOUNT OF THE SUN
MOUNT OF SATURN
MOUNT OF JUPITER
MOUNT OF UPPER MARS
PALM
MOUNT OF LOWER MARS
MOUNT OF THE MOON
MOUNT OF VENUS

PREDOMINANT MOUNT OF VENUS

Physical traits The Venusian is likely to be of above average height with a round face, large, clear eyes, small mouth, thick lips, white teeth and small ears. They will have a high instep, small ankles and long thighs. Venusian men will usually keep their hair until late in life.

▲ Alma-Tadema's painting, The Years at the Spring, *has a sensual feel and shows a woman with large, clear eyes and a small, full mouth. She is a typical Venusian, who tend to be life's romantics.*

Health Strong and healthy, with a cheerful disposition.
Mental and moral character Venusians are happy and sensually inclined people who love life and social interaction. They are the souls of kindness, and hate quarrelling, strife and warfare.

PREDOMINANT MOUNT OF THE MOON

Physical traits Individuals with a predominant mount of the Moon tend to be tall, with a round head and broad forehead. They have very fine hair and hardly any body hair. Large, yellowish teeth, a small mouth with thick, full lips and large, round bulging eyes are all typical characteristics of these individuals.

▼ *Lunar subjects can be ethereal, both emotionally and physically. The moon maiden in this painting by Botticelli,* La Primavera, *has a delicate air.*

Health Lunar subjects are constantly anxious about their health. They suffer from poor circulation, have bursts of energy followed by a need for rest, and may experience problems with their kidneys or bladder.

Mental and moral character Moon subjects are charming and live their life to the full. They are fond of travel and new and exciting experiences, but also enjoy relaxation. They have a fickle nature, and will tend to start a new job before completing the previous one.

PREDOMINANT MOUNT OF MARS

Physical traits Martians tend to be of above average height with a strong bone structure; most noticeably they have prominent cheekbones. They have a large mouth and eyes, thin lips, small, yellowish teeth and small ears. Their head may be proportionally small and the nose may be beak-like. Their voice is powerful and attracts attention.

Health Their fiery temperament may lead to a fever. With this heated character, Martians are at a great risk of accidental injury while arguing.

▲ *The character in Lord Leighton's painting,* La Nanna, *looks strong and striking. She has a typical Martian's strong bone structure, large eyes and prominent nose.*

Mental and moral character Martians are amorous individuals by nature with a generous personality and enjoy social occasions. They can be domineering, and will not listen to reason. They are courageous but not vicious.

PREDOMINANT MOUNT OF MERCURY

Physical traits The Mercurian is small in stature with good bone structure. They stay young-looking longer than others. Their hair is curly and the skin is soft. They have deep-set, penetrating eyes, a long pointed chin and large hands with long thumbs.

▼ *Alma-Tadema's* Portrait of Alice Lewis *captures a Mercurian's intelligent air. Their quick and enquiring mind and even temper makes them excellent judges of other people's character.*

Health The Mercurian is susceptible to a weak liver and digestive organs. They often have a nervous temperament.

Mental and moral character Quick in thought and action, Mercurians are skilful at all games, good students of mathematics and medicine and excellent in business. They are great judges of human character. Usually of an even-tempered nature, they love the closeness of family life. Their acuity and enjoyment of others makes them natural observers and born actors.

PREDOMINANT MOUNT OF THE SUN/APOLLO

Physical traits Solar subjects are usually above average height and shapely. They tend to be muscular and fit, and seldom stocky. Their hair is soft and wavy, their mouth is normal-sized, and they have beautiful, large, almond-shaped eyes.

Health Apollonians, or solar subjects, have good general health. Their eyes are their weak point. Their below-average eyesight may make them prone to silly accidents like tripping over the carpet.

▲ *Sun types can often be found watching people with great interest. Auguste Renoir's painting,* Femme à la Rose, *also shows the solar subject's soft hair and large, almond-shaped eyes.*

Mental and moral character Solar subjects have versatile minds, with clear, logical thought processes and understanding. They love everything that is beautiful in art and nature but are also, in contrast, very competitive and assertive, always wanting to be ahead of the pack. They make an ardent and trustworthy friend but, beware, they can be bitter enemies.

PREDOMINANT MOUNT OF SATURN

Physical traits Saturnians are tall and thin. They have a long face with a pale complexion. Their eyes are deep set and slope downwards so that they appear sad. They have a wide mouth with thin lips, prominent lower jaw, and fine teeth.

▼ *Sensitive Saturnians are often deeply burdened by the sadder side of life. Their physical characteristics emphasise this. Modigliani's painting,* Frans Haellens, *shows the sloping eyes, long face and pale complexion.*

Health These people are susceptible to problems with their legs and feet. They are not keen on drinking plain water, so dehydration may be a problem.

Mental and moral character Saturnians have a certain sadness to their lives. Conservative and suspicious by nature, they dislike taking orders. They are very prudent, born doubters, good problem solvers, and are interested in the occult sciences. They enjoy country life and love solitude. They spend little and save more, but are passionate gamblers. They like dark colours.

PREDOMINANT MOUNT OF JUPITER

Physical traits Jupiterians have a strong bone structure. They are of average height, usually with attractive curves, and they have a stately walk. They tend to have large, deep-set eyes and thick, curly hair. They have a straight nose, full mouth, long teeth, a dimple at the base of the chin and ears close to the head. Jupiterian men may lose their hair at an early age.

Health Jupiterians have a tendency to suffer with digestive problems and will often be overweight.

▲ *Jupiterians have thick curly hair, although the men tend to lose it at an early age. Lord Leighton's* Music *shows a typical Jupiterian straight nose, full mouth and dimpled chin.*

Mental and moral character Destined for public life, Jupiterians have confidence in themselves and can be selfish. They like eating out, most social functions and spend money too freely. They love peace, believe in law and order and are, to a degree, conservative.

THE MOUNTS COMBINED

In some palms two mounts are equally raised. This combination gives you an additional insight into the character of the person whose hand you are reading.

Jupiter and Saturn Excellent luck ahead.
Jupiter and Sun Fame and fortune.
Jupiter and Mercury Love and success in business and science.
Jupiter and upper Mars Bravery and success as a commander.
Jupiter and Moon Imagination.
Jupiter and Venus Pure and respected love towards others.

▲ *Venus (above) and Saturn (below)*

▲ *Jupiter (above) and Mars (left)*

Jupiter and lower Mars Cautiousness.
Saturn and Sun Deep artistic tendencies.
Saturn and Mercury Love of science and nature.
Saturn and upper Mars Argumentative temper.
Saturn and Moon A gift for the occult sciences.
Saturn and Venus Vanity and pride.
Saturn and lower Mars A self-critical and reserved nature.

Sun and Mercury Brilliant talker.
Sun and upper Mars Leadership instincts.

▶ *The Moon*

Sun and Moon Imaginative.
Sun and Venus Love of cultural interests.
Sun and lower Mars Cheerful.

Mercury and upper Mars Logical and strategic.
Mercury and Moon Inventive mind.
Mercury and Venus Prudent and sensible in love.
Mercury and lower Mars Perseverance.

Moon and Venus Looking for the ideal in love.
Upper Mars and Venus Mentality typical of a soldier.

▲ *The Sun (above) and the planet Mercury (below)*

LINES AND SIGNS ON THE MOUNTS

Each mount usually features lines and markings such as crosses, squares, or very strong horizontal lines. These signs give the reader a deeper insight into the person's character than can be found by assessing the dominant mount in isolation. When examining the mounts for these lines and signs, use a magnifying glass to give better definition.

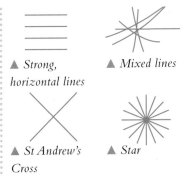

MOUNT OF VENUS

LINES AND SIGNS ON THE MOUNT OF VENUS

Flat, hard mount This marking indicates an individual who has grown cold to love, due to difficulties in past relationships.

Two or three lines This indicates an individual who suffers with ingratitude in love. They believe that they can always do better, hence they can be inconstant in relationships.

▼ *2 or 3 lines*   ▼ *Island*

▲ *Strong, horizontal lines*   ▲ *Mixed lines*

▲ *St Andrew's Cross*   ▲ *Star*

Strong horizontal lines This indicates someone who has an overpowering influence on members of the opposite sex.

Mixed lines This person's disposition will be of a powerfully passionate nature.

Islands Islands in the lines are a sign of someone who has a tendency to feel guilty in love.

▼ *Venus equals love in many languages, even in the language of palmistry.*

St Andrew's Cross A large cross of this type is a sign that there will only ever be one true love in this person's lifetime.

Small cross This indicates a very happy and joyous love affair.

Star by the thumb This indicates a wonderful marriage that will last a lifetime.

Star at base of mount This indicates misfortune for the individual due to the opposite sex, such as divorce or a partner's extreme overspending.

Square at base of mount This person will live a sheltered and protected life.

Triangle This is the mark of someone who is calculating in love: they may marry for money to get ahead.

Grille This is a sign of someone with a dreamy and gentle nature.

▲ *Square*   ▲ *Triangle*

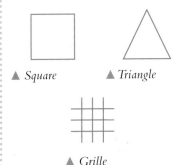

▲ *Grille*

LINES AND SIGNS ON THE MOUNT OF THE MOON

MOUNT OF THE MOON

Long line with a line crossing it Indicates a tendency towards aching bones which could lead to rheumatism.

Cross Indicates a tendency towards heart trouble.

Many lines Indicate a tendency towards insomnia.

Horizontal line The person will be likely to travel.

A voyage line (an angled, horizontal line which reaches up towards the heart line) This individual might suddenly abandon everything to go on a long voyage, or might go to live in another country for reasons of love.

▲ *Horizontal line*

▲ *Ill formed cross* ▲ *Cross*

▲ *Many lines* ▲ *Voyage line*

Mixed lines This, together with a chained heart line, indicates inconsistency in love – the person cannot make up their mind, in matters of love.

Cross This indicates an individual with a superstitious nature.

▼ *When we look at the moon, we are captivated by the mysteries of life.*

Large cross This can indicate an individual who has a tendency to brag a lot.

Cross on upper part of mount This indicates the possibility of trouble with the intestines.

Cross in middle of mount This indicates a tendency towards suffering from rheumatism.

Cross on lower part of mount This cross indicates a tendency towards trouble with the kidneys or possibly with the bladder.

Square This mark signifies protection from bad events throughout a person's life. The greater the number of squares, the greater the luck the individual is likely to have.

Triangle The triangle indicates an individual who has great inner wisdom and creativity.

Grille The grille indicates a tendency towards nerve trouble.

▲ *Mixed lines*

▲ *Grille*

▲ *Square*

▲ *Triangle*

LINES AND SIGNS ON THE MOUNT OF UPPER MARS

One line Indicates an individual with great courage.

Several lines This is someone who may have quite a volatile temper; they can get confused by love, so that they are unable to have a contented relationship.

Horizontal line or lines This indicates a susceptibility to bronchial troubles.

Spot A spot indicates that the individual has been wounded in a fight at some point.

Circle This indicates that the person has been wounded in, or around, the eye.

Square This marking indicates an individual who experiences

MOUNT OF UPPER MARS

▲ *One line*

▲ *Horizontal lines*

▲ *Several lines*

▲ *The god Mars signifies courage and loyalty in abundance; characteristics that are evident in individuals with a line on the mount of upper Mars.*

uncannily good protection from bodily harm.

▲ *Spot*

▲ *Circle*

 ▲ *Square*

 ▲ *Triangle*

Triangle This indicates an individual who is strategically minded, and is especially adept at military operations.

LINES AND SIGNS ON THE MOUNT OF LOWER MARS

Ill-formed cross This marking may indicate that the individual seriously considered suicide in their youth.

Star on horizontal line This indicates an individual who has experienced a great misfortune, or the death of a close relation or friend, in their youth. A marking on the mount of lower Mars is not as auspicious.

MOUNT OF LOWER MARS

▲ *Ill formed cross*

▲ *Star on horizontal line*

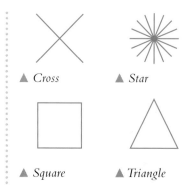

LINES AND SIGNS ON THE MOUNT OF MERCURY

MOUNT OF MERCURY

One line This is a good marking to have. Unexpected financial good fortune will come to this lucky person in the form of a windfall, a lottery win, or an inheritance.

One deep line This marking shows great scientific aptitude: this person is set to carry out valuable research or make an important scientific discovery.

Three or more lines together These multiple lines indicate an individual who has a great interest in medicine and its various, related schools of study.

Mixed lines This individual is, financially, very shrewd and good at saving money to the extent that they may have great difficulty in spending it.

Mixed lines below the heart line The opposite of the example, above, this individual is so generous that they have a tendency to spend too much on others. They should try to curb their desire to spend.

Cross This person has a tendency to deceive, though not always in a

▼ *Good fortune in the form of a lottery win or an unexpected inheritance may come to a person who has a line on the mount of Mercury.*

▲ *One line*   ▲ *One deep line*

▲ *Three lines*   ▲ *Mixed lines*

▲ *Cross*   ▲ *Star*

▲ *Square*   ▲ *Triangle*

negative manner. Sometimes you will see this mark on the palms of actors or sales executives, people who sometimes need to present an image which is not their own. However, people who are prone to lying a great deal can also have this marking.

Star This individual definitely has difficulty telling the truth. More often than not they will be dishonest in their dealings.

Square The individual with this marking is blessed. They will be saved or preserved from heavy financial losses. This is a wonderful marking to have.

Triangle This individual is shrewd in politics and in their dealings with others. They tend to listen first and then respond, and they will usually do so with tact and diplomacy.

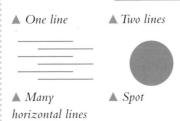

LINES AND SIGNS ON THE MOUNT OF THE SUN

One line This marking is a fortunate one and indicates the likelihood of gaining great wealth.

MOUNT OF THE SUN

Two lines These lines indicate real talent but, unfortunately, without achieving much success.

Many horizontal lines This person has artistic tendencies and could be successful in the creative worlds of painting, for example.

Cross This marking indicates the likelihood of success.

Star The star indicates that fame may be nigh but this is only after the individual has taken many risks to achieve this goal.

▼ *Markings on the mount of the Sun may also indicate a vain individual.*

▲ *One line*   ▲ *Two lines*

▲ *Many horizontal lines*   ▲ *Spot*

Spot A spot indicates that a person is in danger of losing their reputation. They must be watchful and careful if they are to avoid this.

Circle This is a very rare mark and indicates great fame.

Square The square indicates an individual who has a great commercial mind.

▲ *Cross*   ▲ *Star*

▲ *Circle*   ▲ *Square*

▲ *Triangle*   ▲ *Grille*

▲ *The brilliant yellow sunflower blooms rapidly and echoes the fast-growing success and likelihood of fame often indicated by the signs on the mount of the Sun.*

Triangle This marking indicates a selfless individual who wants to assist in the success of others.

Grille The grille can indicate that an individual is inclined to vanity because of their good fortune and fame.

47

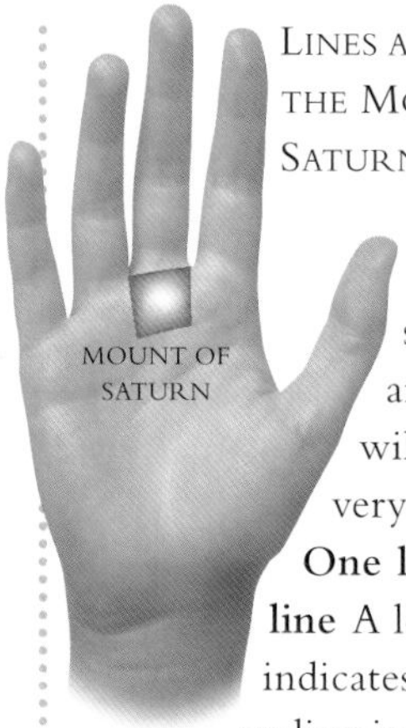

MOUNT OF
SATURN

LINES AND SIGNS ON
THE MOUNT OF
SATURN

One line
A single line
signifies that
an individual
will benefit from
very good luck.
**One long, deep
line** A long, deep line
indicates a peaceful
ending in old age,
perhaps passing away quietly
while sleeping.
Three or more lines This
marking indicates bad luck. The
more lines on the individual's
hand, then the more bad luck
they are likely to face.
Circle A circle is a good marking
to have. It indicates good luck,
and protection from most
troubles in life.
Square A square signifies good
protection from accidents. For

▲ *Most lines on the mount of Saturn
are good omens indicating fortune or
inner wisdom and strength. A
triangle, in particular, is likely to be
found on the hand of someone
spiritual and calm who radiates an
inner peace.*

example, this individual could
emerge from an accident without
a scratch.
Triangle A triangle indicates an
individual who possesses great
inner wisdom and strength.

▲ *One line*   ▲ *One long, deep
line*

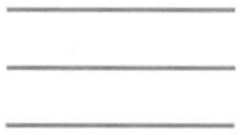

▲ *3 or more lines*    ▲ *Circle*

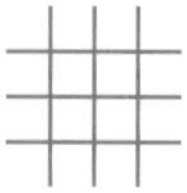

Grille A grille is a negative
marking here. It indicates
someone who is likely to lose
their luck, especially in old age.

▲ *Grille*   ▲ *Square*

▲ *Triangle*

MOUNT OF
JUPITER

LINES AND SIGNS ON THE MOUNT OF JUPITER

Two lines This marking indicates an individual whose ambitions are divided; they are likely to be confused over which path to follow.

Line crossing heart line This indicates that the individual is likely to suffer misfortunes in love.

Cross The cross is a desirable marking. It indicates a very happy relationship where commitment is usually involved.

Cross and star This is the "soulmate" marking: it shows that the individual has found or will find their partner for life.

Star The star marking on the mount indicates a satisfying and sudden rise to fame in life.

Square This indicates an individual who has a natural

▲ *Line crossing heart line*   ▲ *Star*

▲ *Cross*   ▲ *Grille*

▲ *Square*   ▲ *Triangle*

capacity to lead or command. They may follow a military path or be a teacher.

Triangle This marking indicates an individual who is extremely clever and diplomatic. It might be found on the palm of a successful business executive politician or world leader.

Grille This marking indicates an individual who tries too hard to please everyone.

▼ *A cross and a star together on the mount of Jupiter indicate someone who will meet a life-long partner, perhaps even their "soulmate".*

THE MOUNTS AND FINGER TYPES COMBINED

The dominance of a particular mount, in combination with the shape of the fingers, shows up additional aspects of an individual's character to the palm reader. These additional aspects are explored in the tables below and on the following pages.

THE MOUNT OF VENUS

Fingers:	pointed	conical	square	spatulate
normal mount	Believes in love and romance.	Materially minded. Desires security.	Loves family and loves life.	Good comrade and a loyal friend and family member.
raised mount	Imaginative with a creative mind.	Inconsistent in decision making.	Sensual taste in food, music and love.	A love in every port. Not good at stable relationships.
concave mount	Above love. Aloof. Prefers mental activity to physical.	Artistic and creative in nature.	Indifferent to the opposite sex.	Finds opposite sex an encumbrance and is easily annoyed by them.

THE MOUNT OF THE MOON

Fingers:	pointed	conical	square	spatulate
normal mount	Good imagination.	Artistic and visually creative.	Loves poetry and romantic literature.	Loves nature. Hates confined spaces.
raised mount	Emotionally fragile and easily offended.	Extravagant and a spendthrift.	Lacks commonsense. A daydreamer.	Often violent. Prone to overreacting emotionally.
concave mount	(This is never seen.)	An actor or good public speaker.	Has a humdrum existence. Accepts their lot in life.	Never asks "What if?"

Look carefully to see if the mount is average, raised or concave and compare with the finger shape that appears most frequently on the individual's hand. Finger shapes generally fall into one of four main categories – pointed, conical, square and spatulate. You can find illustrations of the four main finger shapes in an earlier section: General Aspects of the Hand.

THE MOUNT OF UPPER MARS

Fingers:	pointed	conical	square	spatulate
normal mount	Courage of the martyr.	Courage of the patriot.	Courage of the soldier.	Courage of the explorer.
raised mount	Religious persecutor. Judgemental of other people.	Vain. Needs lots of attention.	Scheming in business and in love. A manipulator.	A ruffian. A real rogue or heartbreaker.
concave mount	Cowardly by nature and afraid of verbal conflicts.	Cowardly by nature and afraid of verbal conflicts.	Cowardly by nature and afraid of verbal conflicts.	Cowardly in battle and afraid of physical pain.

THE MOUNT OF MERCURY

Fingers:	pointed	conical	square	spatulate
normal mount	Intuitive, even quite psychic.	Eloquent in speech. Stylish by nature.	Great inventor.	Great discoverer.
raised mount	Dreamer of new religions and philosophies.	An inventor of practical things for personal use.	Dangerous schemer, both in business and in love.	Adventurer who stops at nothing.
concave mount	Humane and caring. Loves all life forms.	Has physical or mental difficulties.	No business ability. Not inclined to be self-employed.	Active physically. Always busy.

THE MOUNT OF THE SUN/APOLLO

Fingers:	pointed	conical	square	spatulate
normal mount	Dreamer in life and love.	Idealistic artist or writer. A puritan.	Artist of high standard. A perfectionist.	Drawn to excitement and intrigue.
raised mount	Genius. Eccentric by nature.	Talented in all areas of interest. Competitive.	Stifles real talent. Afraid of own success.	Untalented braggart. Always busy.
concave mount	Art has no place in their life. Practically minded and down to earth.	Clever rather than gifted. Knows how to get ahead by useful associations.	Doesn't care for intellectual pursuits.	Dislikes cultural pursuits. Prefers physical activity.

THE MOUNT OF SATURN

Fingers:	pointed	conical	square	spatulate
normal mount	Poetic in speech and manner.	Morbid. Tends to stress the negative and ignore the positive.	Loves solitude and tranquillity. Doesn't like crowds.	Loves nature and loves life. Has a positive attitude and is fun to be around.
raised mount	Morbid. Tends to stress the negative.	Loves fine art and history.	Dislikes humankind. Prefers nature.	Aggressive and touchy but very loyal.
concave mount	Cynical. Doesn't want to trust others.	Realist in art. Looks for the practical solution.	Indifferent to most things in life.	Cares little for society. Prefers a select group of friends.

THE MOUNT OF JUPITER

Fingers:	pointed	conical	square	spatulate
normal mount	High religious ideals. Looks for the best in others.	Proud with a very loyal nature.	Proud with a very practical nature.	Enterprising in business. Calculating in love.
raised mount	Superstitious. Curious about the esoteric arts.	A perfectionist in artistic and cultural pursuits.	Vain. Sensitive to others' opinions.	Boastful. Not sensitive to others' feelings.
concave mount	Lacking in respect. Too self-interested.	No respect for others. Has difficulties dealing with people.	No self-respect. Allow others to run their lives.	Vulgar. Their actions can offend.

THE MOUNT OF LOWER MARS

Fingers:	pointed	conical	square	spatulate
normal mount	Cautious. Likes to wait and see.	Stoical. Has a very serious nature.	Patient. Enjoys helping others.	Ignores pain and fear. Has a strong personality.
raised mount	Unhealthy. Prone to colds and flu.	Hard-hearted. Afraid to love.	Passively cruel. Secretly likes to see others struggle.	Cruel and cold. Unchangeable.
concave mount	Sensitive soul. Very sweet minded.	Easily offended. Cares too much for the opinion of others.	Afraid of moral and physical pain.	Cowardly by nature. Dislikes conflict.

THE FINGERS AND THUMB

The settings, spacings and patterns on the fingers and thumb show the palm-reader the public persona of the individual. This is the personality that they choose to show to the outside world.

FINGER SETTINGS
The setting of the fingers on the palm varies. They form a distinct shape at the point where they meet the palm.

▼ Fingers set straight across. *This person is self-confident, with plenty of drive. They can be pushy and feel that whatever they do must be automatically right.*

▲ Fingers forming a pitch roof. *This person has a grudge against other people and an inferiority complex. They lack trust in others and self-confidence in themselves.*

◄ Fingers set straight across; little finger dropped down. *When only the little finger is low-set, it is an indication of someone who lacks self-confidence.*

◄ Fingers arched. *These are the fingers of a well-balanced individual, with moderate and tolerant views.*

FINGER SPACINGS

The fingers often incline in one of several patterns. It is worth observing this natural spacing of the fingers for an additional character insight.

◄ Fingers all held apart. *These are the fingers of someone who is extrovert, vivacious, and alert to life's opportunities.*

► Fingers form a pacifier. *This indicates someone who enjoys security and the company of others. They love domestic peace and harmony.*

▲ Fingers held tight together. *This indicates a reserved individual.*

► Fingers divided in the middle. *Those who have this type of hand are resourceful and work well by themselves. They are generally loners in life.*

▲ First finger is set to one side. *This person is intellectually independent.*

► Little finger is set to one side. *This person has a need for physical independence and personal freedom.*

THE SETTINGS OF THE THUMB

The thumb is, if you like, the leader of the hand; it covers the fingers tightly when we clench our fists.

The characteristics of the thumb indicate the strength of a person's conviction and their powers of logic. Measure and compare the phalanges (joint settings) of the thumb. The top section relates to willpower and the second section to reasoning

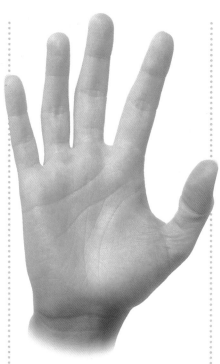

▲ The wider the opening of the thumb (its placement) the more open and trusting the individual.

◄ It is desirable to have a fairly even balance of willpower with reasoning capability. Where one of these areas is lacking, it suggests that the individual will usually be weak in that area: a thumb with a comparatively short first section, for example, would indicate poor willpower. The third indicates the level of an individual's desire and the tendency to act on it.

WILL

REASON

DESIRE

▲ A thumb that is placed close in to the hand indicates an introverted and mistrusting character.

and logic. The mount of Venus will usually be equal to the first and second sections measured together.

A thumb that is set low in the hand (close to the base of the wrist) indicates a practical and cautious person. A thumb that is set high in the hand indicates an individual with a passionate approach to life.

THE PHALANGES OF THE FINGERS

It is important to look for overall balance between the phalanges (joint settings). The first phalanx deals with the mind; the second deals with personal ambitions; and the third deals with desires. If one phalanx in any finger appears excessively long, use the table, opposite, to interpret this characteristic.

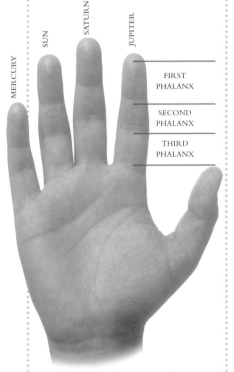

	Jupiter	Saturn	Sun/Apollo	Mercury
long first phalanx	Superstitious. Is interested in the esoteric.	Emotionally fragile. Needs peace of mind.	Artistic tendencies. Has a strong visual sense.	Lying disposition. Finds honesty difficult.
long second phalanx	Vain. Needs the approval of others.	Cautious in business. Respects money.	Inspiration held in check. Sober ego.	Manipulative with a strategic nature.
long third phalanx	Love of power taken too far.	Greedy. Never satisfied with their lot.	Foolish. Needy and clinging.	Always wants what they don't have.

◀ *The phalanges of the Jupiter, Saturn, Apollo and Mercury fingers show up an individual's intellect, personal ambition and desires. Check carefully to see if one phalanx is excessively long in relation to the others.*

▶ *An elongated first phalanx on the Saturn finger can indicate a sensitive individual who feels life's knocks deeply and longs for peace of mind.*

FINGERTIP PATTERNS

When looking at the fingertip and thumb-tip patterns make sure you have good lighting. Use a magnifying glass if it helps. You should interpret the pattern that occurs most frequently.

THE "PEACOCK'S EYE"

This is a rare pattern to find. If it is on the Sun/Apollo finger it guarantees protection from accidental death. On other fingers, it shows a high degree of perception or intuition.

▼ *The peacock's distinctive tail echoes the swirling fingertip pattern called, of course, the peacock's eye.*

▲ *The lines of the tented arch erupt upwards like smoke from the centre of a volcano.*

THE "TENTED ARCH"

This is the least common pattern, and is usually only found on the index finger, if at all. Four examples on ten fingers would be a high count. It suggests emotional sensitivity which verges on instability. This person is very sensitive to stimuli and needs peaceful surroundings. Artistic and idealistic, they have impulsive tendencies. They are highly strung and predisposed to nervous disorders.

THE WHORL

This pattern can be found on any finger or the thumb, but is most often seen on the Sun/Apollo finger. On the thumb, it indicates stubbornness and dogmatism; someone who will not back down even when they have been proved wrong.

On the Sun/Apollo finger, it shows a fine sense of discrimination, with fixed likes and dislikes in such things as clothes and food. It indicates a nonconformist who individualizes everything. They are prone to nervous digestive troubles, heart disease and other nervous disorders.

▼ *The circular swirls of the whorl look like the centre of a whirlpool.*

THE ARCH

The arch is not often found. Prominence of this pattern indicates that an individual may have built a bridge to cross the gap between themselves and the rest of the world. They have a need to provide security for the family and the community. Dedication and loyalty are their watchwords. Their chosen path is that of the saint. They have a predisposition to digestive weaknesses, ulcers and blood disorders.

▼ *The old stone bridge has a gentle curve like the arch.*

▲ *The swirling "S" shape of the composite loop resembles a snake poised to attack.*

THE COMPOSITE LOOP

These two loops reflect two paths to choose from, and indicate an indecisive individual who will weigh up a problem for hours. The pattern is most often found on the thumb or index finger: indecisiveness will be greater if it is on the thumb. The person has a practical and material mind, but can be inflexible, repressive, critical and resentful. There is a predisposition to malignant conditions and mental troubles.

THE LOOP

This is the most commonly found of all patterns and is also known as the "Lunar loop" because it points in the direction of the Moon side of the hand. This marking indicates adaptability and versatility in the face of changing circumstances.

People with this pattern predominating are emotionally responsive and not confined by a narrow viewpoint. They have broad horizons and liberal ideas.

▼ *The sharp curve of a rip curl echoes the shape of the loop.*

FROM THEORY TO PRACTICE

The palm-reader analyses the fingers, the lines and markings on the palm and the actual size and shape of the hands. Anyone can learn to interpret these features, but because there is a lot of information to remember it will take a lot of time and practice. A good palm-reader is one who also brings intuition and common sense to their reading. You are dealing with a whole person, and that includes their feelings. This section is designed to help you understand what will be going through your mind as you read a palm, and how to communicate it with sensitivity.

You may want to gather together a magnifying glass, a pen to mark up lines on the hands and a book to jot down your observations as you go along. A ruler can be useful to work out the proportions of the hand accurately and a pair of compasses will help you mark on the maps of time, if desired.

◀ *In the private time before the palm reading begins, clear your mind and gather your thoughts, so that you can focus your whole attention and intuition on your client.*

▶ *Take your time to scan the hand, noting its size and proportions, before inspecting the lines more closely. Take note of any unusual lines or markings that are obvious on first inspection. These will help to shape the person's character.*

• To begin, take a moment before the other person enters the room. Clear your mind and take several deep breaths.

• Invite the other person in. Focus on your unity with them. Maintain a calm silence until you feel ready to begin. Then explain briefly that the lines and mounts can change, so that everyone has control over their own life. Ask your subject if they are right- or left-handed and how old they are.

• While you are looking at the hands, keep half your attention focused in on your intuition and half of it focused out towards the hands. Maintaining a calm silence, scan the hand noting the relative strength of the mounts and the length of the fingers, including the relative lengths of the three phalanges.

• Also look for the main lines, noticing from where they originate and to where they carry the energy.

• Look for special marks: healing marks, the girdle of Venus, the ring of Solomon, marriage or union lines.

• Ask yourself what the main themes of this person's life are.

• After looking at, and listening to, everything, take a deep breath and let the information come together in your mind.

• You don't have to force it. It will come to you naturally.

◀ *It may help to use a magnifying glass initially, to ensure that you can see all the lines and markings clearly. It will be especially useful in detecting the really fine lines of the typical water hand.*

▶ *Don't hesitate to take notes during the reading. There is a lot to take in, and your notes will be a useful prompt when you draw all the information, and your observations, together later on.*

• When you have a general idea of what you're going to say, assess the person and decide on the best way to express yourself to them; remember, BE KIND!

• Continue to keep half your attention focused in on your intuition and half focused towards the other person.

• Tell them what the palm told you, speaking slowly and clearly. Let your intuition guide

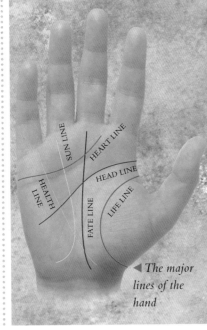

◄ *The major lines of the hand*

you as you decide where to begin. Ask if they understand you. Every hand is unique, every reading takes place at a unique meeting point of time, space and mind. There is no set pattern to follow.

• As long as you touch on the meanings of all the major lines and mounts in the context of the hand, you will do fine.

• Ask yourself: does this person understand what I am saying? Is what I am saying appropriate to their life now? Listen for the answers to these questions in your heart, not in your head.

• Be sure that what you say is exactly what you mean. Open up your intuition and listen to what the palm is telling you. Think carefully and relay this information clearly and with sensitivity.

• Ask the person if they have any further questions. See if the questions can be answered directly from the palm.

• As long as you make it clear that the hands represent probabilities, not certainties, and that the person's lines can often alter with time, you can answer the questions.

• If a person asks about death, or seems to be asking you to take responsibility for major life decisions, do not answer the question directly. Bear in mind that you are not a therapist.

• Above all, take your time and keep yourself open and receptive to your intuition.

• Once you have gone over all that you have seen in their hand, bring the reading slowly to a close.

• Take time once your client has left to go over your reading in your mind. Was there any thing else you could have said?

► *An old woodcut of a palm shows the intricate nature of this ancient practice, and also how little it has changed over the years.*

FURTHER INFORMATION

FROM THE AUTHOR

Palmistry has been studied and practised by all the female members of my family for many generations. As a result of this long matrilineal line I have arrived at this point in my own study of palmistry. Together with my work with David, my co-author, and my work at my shop *Way Out There and Back*, this lineage has enabled me to research and develop this form of divination on a practical level for use in many arenas in conjunction with our modern, everyday lives. It is my aim to offer people the springboard to gain insights and learn from the wisdom of the East and the New Age as well as my own experience of working in this field, to help them to further their own studies of palmistry.

I would like to thank the students who have studied with me, both past and present. And finally, I would like to thank all the readers of this book.

Good luck!

Staci Mendoza

FIND OUT MORE

Personalised palm charts are available from:

Way Out There and Back
20 Evans Gardens
Arcade Road
Littlehampton
West Sussex
BN17 5AP
tel. 01903 722666
email: wotab@mistral.co.uk
URL: www.wotab.co.uk

PICTURE CREDITS

The majority of photographs in this book were taken by John Freeman. The publishers would also like to thank the following picture libraries for supplying images:
Images Colour Library pages 2, 8 (bl, tr), 21 (tl, br) 25 (tr), 42 (tm), 44 (bm)
e.t. archive page 9
Super Stock pages 7 (br), 11 (bm), 14 (br), 23 (br), 27 (bl), 33 (tr), 35 (tl), 49 (bl)
Tony Stone Images page 6 (tr), 7 (tl), 26 (tr), 27 (tr), 29 (tr), 31 (bl, br), 34 (bl), 36 (tr), 42 (lm, bl), 42 (mr, m, tr), 46 (bm), 47 (tr), 57 (br), 58 (bl, br), 59 (bl, tm, br)
Mary Evans Picture Library page 23 (tl)
The Bridgeman Art Library page 47 (bl)
Planet Earth Pictures pages 28 (tr), 42 (br), 58 (mt)
The Stock Market (International) pages 6 (bl, br), 11 (tr), 25 (bl), 33 (tr)
Houses and Interiors page 12 (tr)
Fine Art Photographic Library Ltd pages 24 (tr), 38 (tr), 39 (tr), 41 (tr), 43 (bm)
AKG Photo London pages 39 (bl), 40 (bl), 40 (tr).

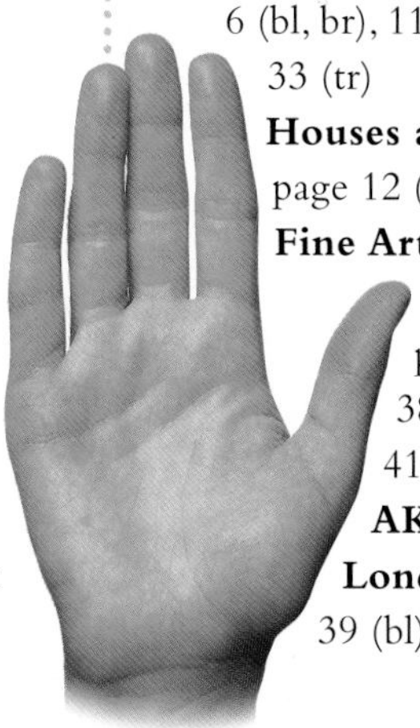

INDEX

air hand, 16

bars and dots, 30

chains, 31
circles, 31
conical hand, 10
crosses, 30

earth hand, 17
elemental hands, 16–17

fate line, 19, 26–7
fingers: phalanges, 57
   settings, 54
   shapes, 12
   spacings, 55
fingertip patterns, 58–9
fire hand, 17
forks, 31

head line, 18, 22–3
heart line, 18–19, 24–5
history, 8–9

islands, 31

Jupiter, mount of, 40, 49, 53

life line, 18, 20–1
lines: major lines, 18–29
   on mounts, 43–9

maps of time, 32–3
marks on lines, 30–1
marriage lines, 36
Mars: Mars line, 34
   mount of, 39, 45, 51, 53
   plain of, 36
medical stigmata, 35
Mercury: Mercury line, 19, 29
   mount of, 40, 46, 51
Moon, mount of, 39, 44, 50
mounts, 38–53
mystic cross, 36

palm edge, 37
percussive edge, 37
phalanges, 57
plain of Mars, 36
pointed hand, 10
proportions of hand, 11

rascettes, 34
readings, 60–2

Saturn: mount of, 40, 48, 52
   ring of, 35
shape of fingers, 12
shape of hand, 10
signs, on mounts, 43–9
size of hand, 14–15
Solomon, ring of, 35
spatulate hand, 10
special-interest lines, 34–6
square hand, 10
squares, 30
stars, 31
Sun: Sun line, 19, 28
   mount of, 40, 47, 52
sympathy lines, 35

tassels, 31
thickness of hand, 13
thumb, 56
time maps, 32–3

Venus: girdle of, 34–5
   mount of, 38, 43, 50

water hand, 16

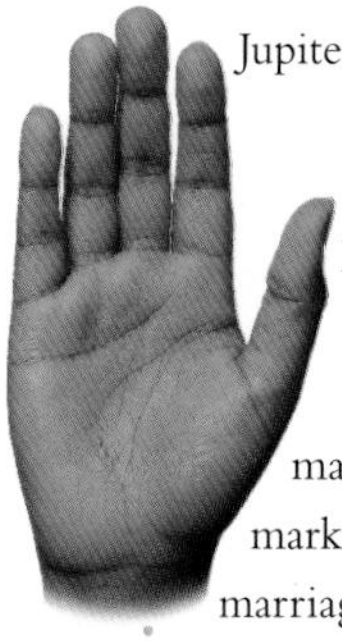